Contents

Section 1: Introduction

What is an Approved Document?

1.1   This Approved Document, which takes effect on 1 October 2010 has been approved and issued by the Secretary of State to provide practical guidance on ways of complying with the *energy efficiency requirements* (see Section 2) and regulation 7 of the Building Regulations 2010 (SI 2010/2214) for England and Wales. Regulation 2(1) of the Building Regulations defines the *energy efficiency requirements* as the requirements of regulations 23, 25A, 25B, 26, 28, 29 and 40 and Part L of Schedule 1. The Building Regulations 2010 are referred to throughout the remainder of this Document as 'the Building Regulations'.

1.2   The intention of issuing Approved Documents is to provide guidance about compliance with specific aspects of building regulations in some of the more common building situations. They set out what, in ordinary circumstances, may be accepted as reasonable provision for compliance with the relevant requirement(s) of building regulations to which they refer.

1.3   If guidance in an Approved Document is followed there will be a presumption of compliance with the requirement(s) covered by the guidance. However, this presumption can be overturned, so simply following guidance does not guarantee compliance; for example, if the particular case is unusual in some way, then 'normal' guidance may not be applicable. It is also important to note that there may well be other ways of achieving compliance with the requirements. **There is therefore no obligation to adopt any particular solution contained in this Approved Document if you would prefer to meet the relevant requirement in some other way. Persons intending to carry out building work should always check with their building control body, either the local authority or an approved inspector, that their proposals comply with building regulations.**

1.4   It is important to note that this Approved Document, as well as containing guidance, also contains extracts from the Regulations. Such regulatory text must be complied with as stated. For example, the requirement that *fixed building services* must be commissioned (regulation 44) is a regulatory requirement. There is therefore no flexibility to ignore this requirement; neither can compliance with this particular regulation be demonstrated via any route other than that set out in regulation 44.

1.5   The guidance contained in this Approved Document relates only to the particular requirements of the Building Regulations that the document addresses (set out in Section 2). However, building work may be subject to more than one requirement of building regulations. In such cases the work will also have to comply with any other applicable requirements of building regulations.

1.6   There are Approved Documents that give guidance on each of the Parts of Schedule 1 and on regulation 7. A full list of these is provided at the back of this document.

Consideration of technical risk

1.7   Building work to existing *dwellings* must satisfy all the technical requirements set out in regulations 23, 22, 28 and 29 of, and Schedule 1 to, the Building Regulations. When considering the incorporation of energy efficiency measures in *dwellings*, attention should also be paid in particular to the need to comply with Part B (fire safety), Part C (site preparation and resistance to contaminants and moisture), Part E (resistance to the passage of sound), Part F (ventilation), paragraph G3 (hot water supply and systems), Part J (combustion appliances and fuel storage systems) and Part P (electrical safety) of Schedule 1 to the Building Regulations, as well as Part L. The adoption of any particular energy efficiency measure should not involve unacceptable technical risk of, for instance, excessive condensation. Designers and builders should refer to the relevant Approved Documents and to other generally available good practice guidance to help minimise these risks.

How to use this Approved Document

1.8   This Approved Document is subdivided into seven sections as detailed below. These sections are followed by supporting appendices.

This **introductory** section sets out the general context in which the guidance in this Approved Document must be considered.

Section 2 sets out the relevant legal requirements contained in the Building Regulations.

Section 3 contains general guidance, including the definition of key terms, the types of building work covered by this Approved Document, the types of building work that are exempt, procedures for notifying work, materials and workmanship and health and safety issues.

Section 4 gives guidance on reasonable provision for various types of building work.

Section 5 deals with the particular case of work to *thermal elements*.

Section 6 gives guidance in support of the requirement for *consequential improvements* for buildings over 1,000 m².

Section 7 describes the information that should be provided to occupiers to help them achieve reasonable standards of energy efficiency in practice.

1.9 In this document the following conventions have been adopted to assist understanding and interpretation:

a. Texts shown against a green background are extracts from the Building Regulations 2010 (SI 2010/2214) or Building (Approved Inspectors etc.) Regulations 2010 (SI 2010/2215) and set out the legal requirements that relate to compliance with the *energy efficiency requirements* of building regulations. As stated previously, there is no flexibility in respect of such text; it defines a legal requirement, not guidance for typical situations. It should also be remembered that, as noted above, building works must comply with all the other applicable requirements of building regulations.

b. Key terms are defined in paragraph 3.1 and are printed in ***bold italic text***.

c. Details of technical publications referred to in the text of this Approved Document will be given in footnotes and repeated as references at the end of the document. A reference to a publication is likely to be made for one of two main reasons. The publication may contain additional or more comprehensive technical detail, which it would be impractical to include in full in the Approved Document but which is needed to fully explain ways of meeting the requirements; or it is a source of more general information. The reason for the reference will be indicated in each case. The reference will be to a specified edition of the document. The Approved Document may be amended from time to time to include new references or to refer to revised editions where this aids compliance.

d. Additional *commentary in italic text* appears after some numbered paragraphs. This commentary is intended to assist understanding of the immediately preceding paragraph or sub-paragraph, or to direct readers to sources of additional information, but is not part of the technical guidance itself.

Where you can get further help

1.10 If you do not understand the technical guidance or other information set out in this Approved Document and the additional detailed technical references to which it directs you, there are a number of routes through which you can seek further assistance:

- the Department for Communities and Local Government website: www.gov.uk;

- the Planning Portal website: www.planningportal.gov.uk;

- if you are the person undertaking the building work, you can seek assistance either from your local authority building control service or from your approved inspector (depending on which building control service you are using;

- persons registered with a competent person self-certification scheme may be able to get technical advice from their scheme operator;

- if your query is of a highly technical nature, you may wish to seek the advice of a specialist, or industry technical body, for the relevant subject.

Responsibility for compliance

1.11 It is important to remember that if you are the person (e.g. designer, builder, installer) carrying out building work to which any requirement of building regulations applies you have a responsibility to ensure that the work complies with any such requirement. The building owner may also have a responsibility for ensuring compliance with building regulation requirements and could be served with an enforcement notice in cases of non-compliance.

Section 2: The requirements

2.1   This Approved Document, which takes effect on 1 October 2010, deals with the *energy efficiency requirements* in the Building Regulations. Regulation 2(1) of the Building Regulations defines the *energy efficiency requirements* as the requirements of regulations 23, 25A, 25B, 26, 28, 29 and 40 and Part L of Schedule 1. The *energy efficiency requirements* relevant to this Approved Document, which deals with existing *dwellings*, are those in regulations 23, 28, 29 and 40 of, and Part L of Schedule 1 to, those Regulations and are set out below.

Requirements for the renovation or replacement of thermal elements – Regulation 23

(1) Where the renovation of an individual thermal element—

   (a) constitutes a major renovation; or

   (b) amounts to the renovation of more than 50% of the element's surface area;

   the renovation must be carried out so as to ensure that the whole of the element complies with paragraph L1(a)(i) of Schedule 1, in so far as that is technically, functionally and economically feasible.

(2) Where the whole or any part of an individual element is proposed to be replaced and the replacement—

   (a) constitutes a major renovation; or

   (b) (in the case of part replacement) amounts to the replacement of more than 50% of the thermal element's surface area;

   the whole of the thermal element must be replaced so as to ensure that it complies with paragraph L1(a)(i) of Schedule 1, in so far as that is technically, functionally and economically feasible.

Consequential improvements to energy performance Regulation 28

(1) Paragraph (2) applies to an existing building with a total useful floor area over 1000 m² where the proposed building work consists of or includes—

   (a) an extension;

   (b) the initial provision of any fixed building services; or

   (c) an increase to the installed capacity of any fixed building services.

(2) Subject to paragraph (3), where this paragraph applies, such work, if any, shall be carried out as is necessary to ensure that the building complies with the requirements of Part L of Schedule 1.

(3) Nothing in paragraph (2) requires work to be carried out if it is not technically, functionally or economically feasible.

Energy Performance Certificates – Regulation 29

(1) This regulation applies where—

(a) a building is erected; or

(b) a building is modified so that it has a greater or fewer number of parts designed or altered for separate use than it previously had, where the modification includes the provision or extension of any of the fixed services for heating, hot water, air conditioning or mechanical ventilation.

(2) The person carrying out the work shall—

(a) give an energy performance certificate for the building to the owner of the building; and

(b) give to the local authority notice to that effect, including the reference number under which the energy performance certificate has been registered in accordance with regulation 30(4).

(3) The energy performance certificate and notice shall be given not later than five days after the work has been completed.

(4) The energy performance certificate must—

(a) express the asset rating of the building in a way approved by the Secretary of State under regulation 24;

(b) include a reference value such as a current legal standard or benchmark;

(c) be issued by an energy assessor who is accredited to produce energy performance certificates for the category of building to which the certificate relates;

(cc) include a recommendation report unless there is no reasonable potential for energy performance improvements (in terms of the applicable energy efficiency requirements);

(cd) be valid in accordance with paragraph (9); and

(d) include the following information—

(i) the reference number under which the set of data from which the certificate may be produced has been entered onto the register in accordance with regulation 30(4);

(ii) the address of the building, or in the case of a portable building the address of the owner;

(iii) an estimate of the total useful floor area of the building;

(iv) the name of the energy assessor who issued it;

(v) the name and address of the energy assessor's employer, or, if self-employed, the name under which the assessor trades and the assessor's address;

(vi) the date on which it was issued; and

(vii) the name of the approved accreditation scheme of which the energy assessor is a member.

(5) ...

(6) Certification for apartments or units designed or altered for separate use in blocks may be based—

(a) except in the case of a dwelling, on a common certification of the whole building for blocks with a common heating system; or

(b) on the assessment of another representative apartment or unit in the same block.

Energy performance certificates – Regulation 29 *(continued)*

(7) Where —

(a) a block with a common heating system is divided into parts designed or altered for separate use; and

(b) one or more, but not all, of the parts are dwellings,

certification for those parts which are not dwellings may be based on a common certification of all the parts which are not dwellings.

(8) Certification for a building which consists of a single dwelling may be based on the assessment of another representative building of similar design and size with a similar actual energy performance quality, provided such correspondence is guaranteed by the energy assessor issuing the energy performance certificate.

(9) An energy performance certificate is only valid if—

(a) it was entered on the register no more than 10 years before the date on which it is made available; and

(b) no other energy performance certificate for the building has since been entered on the register.

(10) An energy performance certificate must not contain any information or data (except for the address of the building) from which a living individual (other than the energy assessor or his employer) can be identified.

Recommendation reports – Regulation 29A

29A.—(1) In these Regulations a "recommendation report" means recommendations made by an energy assessor for the cost-effective improvement of the energy performance of a building.

(2) A recommendation report must include—

(a) recommended cost-effective measures that could be carried out in connection with a major renovation of the building envelope or fixed building services;

(b) recommended cost-effective measures for individual building elements that could be carried out without the necessity for a major renovation of the building envelope or fixed building services;

(c) an indication as to how the owner or tenant can obtain more detailed information about improving the energy efficiency of the building, including more detailed information about the cost-effectiveness of the recommendations; and

(d) information on the steps to be taken to implement the recommendations.

(3) Any cost-effective measure which the energy assessor recommends must be technically feasible for the building to which the recommendation report relates.

(4) In this regulation "building element" means a controlled service or fitting or a thermal element of the building envelope.

Requirement	Limits on application

Schedule 1 – Part L Conservation of fuel and power

L1. Reasonable provision shall be made for the conservation of fuel and power in buildings by:

    (a) limiting heat gains and losses—

        (i) through thermal elements and other parts of the building fabric; and

        (ii) from pipes, ducts and vessels used for space heating, space cooling and hot water services;

    (b) providing fixed building services which—

        (i) are energy efficient;

        (ii) have effective controls; and

        (iii) are commissioned by testing and adjusting as necessary to ensure they use no more fuel and power than is reasonable in the circumstances; and

Regulation 40 providing to the owner sufficient information about the building, the fixed building services and their maintenance requirements so that the building can be operated in such a manner as to use no more fuel and power than is reasonable in the circumstances.

LIMITATION ON REQUIREMENTS

2.2 In accordance with regulation 8 of the Building Regulations, the requirements in Parts A to D and F to K (except for paragraphs G2, H2 and J7) of Schedule 1 to the Building Regulations do not require anything to be done except for the purpose of securing reasonable standards of health and safety for persons in or about buildings (and any others who may be affected by buildings or matters connected with buildings).

2.3 Paragraph G2 is excluded as it deals with water efficiency and paragraphs H2 and J7 are excluded from regulation 8 because they deal directly with prevention of the contamination of water. Parts E and M (which deal, respectively, with resistance to the passage of sound, and access to and use of buildings) are excluded from regulation 8 because they address the welfare and convenience of building users. Part L is excluded from regulation 8 because it addresses the conservation of fuel and power.

2.4 In addition, regulation 4(2) of the Building Regulations states that where the work is being carried out in order to comply with regulation 23 (requirements relating to **renovation** or replacement of a **thermal element**), regulation 22 (requirements relating to a change of a building's energy status) or regulation 28 (**consequential improvements** to energy performance), and is not a material alteration, it need comply only with the requirements of Part L.

Section 3: General guidance

Key terms

3.1   The following are key terms used in this document:

BCB means Building Control Body: a local authority or an approved inspector.

Building envelope in relation to a building means the walls, floor, roof, windows, doors, roof windows and roof-lights.

Commissioning means the advancement of a **fixed building service** following installation, replacement or alteration of the whole or part of the system, from the state of static completion to working order by testing and adjusting as necessary to ensure that the system as a whole uses no more fuel and power than is reasonable in the circumstances, without prejudice to the need to comply with health and safety requirements. For each system **commissioning** includes setting-to-work, regulation (that is testing and adjusting repetitively) to achieve the specified performance, the calibration, setting up and testing of the associated automatic control systems, and recording of the system settings and the performance test results that have been accepted as satisfactory.

Consequential improvements means those energy efficiency improvements required by regulation 28.

Controlled service or fitting means a service or fitting in relation to which Part G (sanitation, hot water safety and water efficiency), H (drainage and waste disposal), J (combustion appliances and fuel storage systems), L (conservation of fuel and power) or P (electrical safety) of Schedule 1 to the Building Regulations imposes a requirement.

Dwelling means a self-contained unit, including a house or a flat, designed to be used separately to accommodate a single household. (**Rooms for residential purposes** are not **dwellings** so Approved Document L2B applies to work in such buildings.)

Energy efficiency requirements means the requirements of regulations 23, 25A, 25B, 26, 28, 29 and 40 of, and Part L of Schedule 1 to, the Building Regulations.

energy performance certificate means a certificate which complies with regulation 29 of these regulations.

*In respect of existing **dwellings** the applicable requirements consist of Part L and regulations 23, 38 and 40.*

Fixed building services means any part of, or any controls associated with—

(a) fixed internal or external lighting systems (but not including emergency escape lighting or specialist process lighting);

(b) fixed systems for heating, hot water, air conditioning or mechanical ventilation; or

(c) any combination of systems of the kinds referred to in paragraph (a) or (b);

Major renovation means the renovation of a building where more than 25% of the surface area of the building envelope undergoes renovation.

Room for residential purposes means a room, or a suite of rooms, which is not a dwelling-house or a flat and which is used by one or more persons to live and sleep and includes a room in a hostel, an hotel, a boarding house, a hall of residence or a residential home, but does not include a room in a hospital, or other similar establishment, used for patient accommodation.

'Renovation' in relation to a thermal element means the provision of a new layer in the thermal element (other than where that new layer is provided solely as a means of repair to a flat roof) or the replacement of an existing layer, but excludes decorative finishes, and 'renovate' shall be construed accordingly.

Simple payback means the amount of time it will take to recover the initial investment through energy savings, and is calculated by dividing the marginal additional cost of implementing an energy efficiency measure by the value of the annual energy savings achieved by that measure taking no account of VAT. When making this calculation the following guidance should be used:

a. the marginal additional cost is the additional cost (materials and labour) of incorporating (e.g.) additional insulation, not the whole cost of the work;

b. the cost of implementing the measure should be based on prices current at the date the proposals are made known to the **BCB** and be confirmed in a report signed by a suitably qualified person;

c. the annual energy savings should be estimated using SAP 2012[1];

d. for the purposes of this Approved Document, the energy prices that are current at the time of the application to building control should be used when evaluating the annual energy savings. Current energy prices can be obtained from the DECC website[2].

---

[1]   www.bre.co.uk/sap2012.

[2]   www.gov.uk/government/organisations/department-of-energy-climate-change/about/statistics#energy-price-statistics.

Thermal element is defined in regulation 2(3) of the Building Regulations as follows:

2(3) In these Regulations 'thermal element' means a wall, floor or roof (but does not include windows, doors, roof windows or roof-lights) which separates a thermally conditioned part of the building ('the conditioned space') from:

a. the external environment (including the ground); or

b. in the case of floors and walls, another part of the building which is:

    i. unconditioned;

    ii. an extension falling within class VII in Schedule 2; or

    iii. where this paragraph applies, conditioned to a different temperature,

and includes all parts of the element between the surface bounding the conditioned space and the external environment or other part of the building as the case may be.

2(4) Paragraph 2(3)(b)(iii) only applies to a building which is not a dwelling, where the other part of the building is used for a purpose which is not similar or identical to the purpose for which the conditioned space is used.

*Note that this definition encompasses the walls and floor of a swimming pool basin where this is part of an existing **dwelling**.*

Types of work covered by this Approved Document

3.2 This Approved Document is intended to give guidance on what, in ordinary circumstances, may be considered reasonable provision for compliance with the requirements of regulation 23 and 28 of, and Part L of Schedule 1 to, the Building Regulations for those carrying out building work to existing **dwellings**. In addition it gives guidance on compliance with regulations 25A, 27, 43 and 44 of the Building Regulations and 20(1), 20(2) and 20(6) of the Approved Inspectors Regulations 2010.

*Buildings exclusively containing **rooms for residential purposes** such as nursing homes, student accommodation and similar are not **dwellings**, and in such cases Approved Document L2B applies.*

3.3 In particular, this Approved Document gives guidance on compliance with the **energy efficiency requirements** where the following occurs:

a. the construction of an extension (see paragraphs 4.1 to 4.9);

b. a material change of use, or a change to the building's energy status, including such work as loft and garage conversions (paragraphs 4.11 to 4.16);

c. the provision or extension of a **controlled service** or **controlled fitting** (paragraphs 4.17 to 4.37);

d. the replacement or **renovation** of a **thermal element** (Section 5);

e. the **major renovation** of a building.

3.4 Where the activities include building work in a **dwelling** that is part of a mixed-use building, account should also be taken of the guidance in Approved Document L2B in relation to those parts of the building that are not **dwellings**, including any common areas.

*It should be noted that **dwellings** are defined as self-contained units. **Rooms for residential purposes** are not **dwellings**, and so Approved Document L2B applies to them.*

Dwellings within the scope of the energy efficiency requirements

3.5 The **energy efficiency requirements** of the Building Regulations apply only to buildings which are roofed constructions having walls and which use energy to condition the indoor climate. For **dwellings** the requirements will apply to:

- the erection of a **dwelling** (guidance on this is given in Approved Document L1A);

- the extension of a **dwelling** other than some extensions falling within Class VII in Schedule 2 to the Building Regulations; or

- the carrying out of any building work to or in connection with an existing **dwelling** or an extension to an existing **dwelling**.

Dwellings exempt from the energy efficiency requirements

3.6 There are two exemptions from the **energy efficiency requirements** that may apply to building work to existing **dwellings** or extensions to existing **dwellings**:

a. Buildings which are:

- listed in accordance with section 1 of the Planning (Listed Buildings and Conservation Areas) Act 1990;

- in a conservation area designated in accordance with section 69 of that Act; or

- included in the schedule of monuments maintained under section 1 of the Ancient Monuments and Archaeological Areas Act 1979.

For these buildings the exemption applies only to the extent that compliance with the **energy efficiency requirements** would unacceptably alter the character or appearance of such existing **dwellings**. Guidance on these buildings is given in paragraphs 3.7 to 3.14 below.

b. Carports, covered yards, covered ways and some conservatories or porches attached to existing **dwellings**. Guidance on these is given at paragraphs 3.15 and 3.16 below.

Historic and traditional buildings which may have an exemption

3.7   As mentioned above in paragraph 3.6a, the following classes of buildings have an exemption from the *energy efficiency requirements* where compliance would unacceptably alter the character or appearance of the buildings.

a. listed buildings;

b. buildings in conservation areas; and

c. scheduled ancient monuments.

Historic and traditional buildings where special considerations may apply

3.8   There are three further classes of buildings where special considerations in making reasonable provision for the conservation of fuel or power may apply:

a. buildings which are of architectural and historical interest and which are referred to as a material consideration in a local authority's development plan or local development framework;

b. buildings which are of architectural and historical interest within national parks, areas of outstanding natural beauty, registered historic parks and gardens, registered battlefields, the curtilages of scheduled ancient monuments, and world heritage sites;

c. buildings of traditional construction with permeable fabric that both absorbs and readily allows the evaporation of moisture.

3.9   When undertaking work on or in connection with a building that falls within one of the classes listed above, the aim should be to improve energy efficiency as far as is reasonably practicable. The work should not prejudice the character of the host building or increase the risk of long-term deterioration of the building fabric or fittings.

3.10   The guidance given by English Heritage[3] should be taken into account in determining appropriate energy performance standards for building work in historic buildings.

In addition English Heritage has produced detailed technical guidance on how to implement specific energy efficiency measures. (See list of available guidance documents at http://www.english-heritage.org.uk/professional/advice/advice-by-topic/climate-change/energy-efficiency/.)

3.11   In general, new extensions to historic or traditional *dwellings* should comply with the standards of energy efficiency as set out in this Approved Document. The only exception would be where there is a particular need to match the external appearance or character of the extension to that of the host building (see paragraph 4.2).

---

[3]   Energy Efficiency and Historic Buildings, English Heritage, 2011
http://www.english-heritage.org.uk/publications/energy-efficiency-historic-buildings-ptl/.

3.12   Particular issues relating to work in historic buildings that warrant sympathetic treatment and where advice from others could therefore be beneficial include:

a. restoring the historic character of a building that has been subject to previous inappropriate alteration, e.g. replacement windows, doors and rooflights;

b. rebuilding a former historic building (e.g. following a fire or filling a gap site in a terrace);

c. making provisions enabling the fabric of historic buildings to 'breathe' to control moisture and potential long-term decay problems.

3.13   In assessing reasonable provision for energy efficiency improvements for historic buildings of the sort described in paragraphs 3.7 and 3.8, it is important that the *BCB* takes into account the advice of the local authority's conservation officer. The views of the conservation officer are particularly important where building work requires planning permission and/or listed building consent.

3.14   Other classes of buildings to which special considerations apply are usually non-domestic in character, and so are covered in ADL2A and ADL2B.

Conservatories and porches

3.15   Regulation 21 of the Building Regulations exempts some conservatory and porch extensions from the *energy efficiency requirements*. The exemption applies only for conservatories or porches:

*   which are at ground level;

*   where the floor area is less than 30 m²;

*   where the glazing complies with Part K 4 of Schedule 1;

*   where the existing walls, doors and windows in the part of the *dwelling* which separates the conservatory are retained or, if removed, replaced by walls, windows and doors which meet the *energy efficiency requirements*; and

*   where the heating system of the *dwelling* is not extended into the conservatory or porch.

3.16   Where any conservatory or porch does not meet all the requirements in the preceding paragraph, it is not exempt and must comply with the relevant *energy efficiency requirements* (see paragraphs 4.8 and 4.9 below).

Notification of work covered by the Energy Efficiency requirements

3.17   In most instances in order to comply with the Building Regulations it will be necessary to notify a *BCB* before the work starts. Where you choose to use the local authority and any work relates to the common parts of a block of flats, this must be by deposit of full plans. For other existing *dwellings* this could be either in the form of a deposit of full plans or by a building notice. There is no set procedure where the *BCB* is an Approved Inspector provided they have been notified at least 5 days before work starting.

3.18 In certain situations, however, you do not need to notify a **BCB**:

a. Where the work is being carried out by a person registered with a relevant competent person self-certification scheme listed in Schedule 3 to the Building Regulations, no advance notification to the **BCB** is needed (see paragraphs 3.19 to 3.22).

b. Where the work involves an emergency repair, e.g. to a failed boiler or a leaking hot water cylinder, in accordance with regulation 12(7) of the Building Regulations there is no need to delay making the repair in order to make an advance notification to the **BCB**. However, in such cases it will still be necessary for the work to comply with the relevant requirements and to give a notice to the **BCB** at the earliest opportunity, unless an installer registered under an appropriate competent person scheme carries out the work. A completion certificate can then be issued in the normal way.

c. Where the work is of a minor nature as described in the schedule of non-notifiable work (Schedule 4 to the Building Regulations), the work must still comply with the relevant requirements but need not be notified to the **BCB** (see paragraphs 3.23 to 3.25).

Competent person self-certification schemes

3.19 It is not necessary to notify a **BCB** in advance of work which is to be carried out by a person registered with a competent person self-certification scheme listed in Schedule 3 to the Building Regulations. In order to join such a scheme a person must demonstrate competence to carry out the type of work the scheme covers, and also the ability to comply with all relevant requirements in the Building Regulations.

3.20 Where work is carried out by a person registered with a competent person scheme, regulation 20 of the Building Regulations 2010 and regulation 20(1) of the Building (Approved Inspectors etc) Regulations 2010 require that the occupier of the building be given, within 30 days of the completion of the work, a certificate confirming that the work complies fully with all applicable building regulation requirements. There is also a requirement to give the **BCB** a notice of the work carried out, again within 30 days of the completion of the work. These certificates and notices are usually made available through the scheme operator.

3.21 **BCBs** are authorised to accept these certificates and notices as evidence of compliance with the requirements of the Building Regulations. Local authority inspection and enforcement powers remain unaffected, although they are normally used only in response to a complaint that work does not comply.

3.22 A list of authorised self-certification schemes and the types of work for which they are authorised can be found at www.communities.gov.uk

Work which need not be notified

3.23 Schedule 4 to the Building Regulations sets out types of work where there is no requirement to notify a **BCB** that work is to be carried out. These types of work are mainly of a minor nature where there is no significant risk to health, safety or energy efficiency. Note that the health, safety and **energy efficiency requirements** continue to apply to these types of work, and that only the need to notify a **BCB** has been removed. In addition, where only non-notifiable work is carried out by a member of a competent person self-certification scheme there is no requirement for a certificate of building regulations compliance to be given to the occupier or the **BCB**.

3.24 The types of non-notifiable work in Schedule 4 relevant to the **energy efficiency requirements** of the Regulations are:

a. In a heating, hot water, ventilation or air-conditioning system, the replacement of any part which is not a combustion appliance (such as a radiator, valve or pump) or the addition of an output device (such as a radiator or fan) or the addition of a control device (such as a thermostatic radiator valve). However, the work will remain notifiable whenever **commissioning** is possible and necessary to enable a reasonable use of fuel and power (see paragraphs 4.30 to 4.37).

b. The installation of a stand-alone, self-contained fixed heating, hot water, ventilation or air-conditioning service. Such services must consist only of a single appliance and any associated controls, and must not be connected to, or form part of, any other **fixed building service**. Examples of non-notifiable services would be a fixed electric heater, a mechanical extractor fan in a kitchen or bathroom, and a room air-conditioning unit. However, if any of the following apply, the work will remain notifiable building work:

　　i. the service is a combustion appliance;

　　ii. any electrical work associated with the installation is notifiable;

　　iii. **commissioning** is possible and would affect the service's energy efficiency (see paragraphs 4.30 to 4.38);

　　iv. in the case of a ventilation appliance, the appliance is installed in a room containing a natural draught open-flued combustion appliance or service, such as a gas fire which uses a chimney as its flue.

c. Installation of thermal insulation in a roof space or loft space where this is the only work carried out and the work is not carried out to comply with any requirement in the Building Regulations, i.e. the work is carried out voluntarily.

3.25 Schedule 4 also sets out what types of electrical installation work in **dwellings** are non-notifiable. Full information on this is given in Approved Document P.

Materials and workmanship

3.26   Any building work which is subject to the requirements imposed by schedule 1 to the Building Regulations shall be carried out in accordance with regulation 7. Guidance on meeting these requirements on materials and workmanship is contained in the Approved Document to support regulation 7.

3.27   Building Regulations are made for specific purposes, primarily the health and safety, welfare and convenience of people and for energy conservation. Standards and other technical specifications may provide relevant guidance to the extent that they relate to these considerations. However, they may also address other aspects of performance or matters which, although they relate to health and safety etc., are not covered by the Building Regulations.

3.28   When an Approved Document makes reference to a named standard, the relevant version of the standard to which it refers is the one listed at the end of the publication. However, if this version has been revised or updated by the issuing standards body, the new version may be used as a source of guidance provided it continues to address the relevant requirements of the Regulations.

The Workplace (Health, Safety and Welfare) Regulations 1992

3.29   The Workplace (Health, Safety and Welfare) Regulations 1992, as amended, apply to the common parts of flats and similar buildings if people such as cleaners, wardens and caretakers are employed to work in these common parts. These Regulations contain some requirements which affect building design. The main requirements are now covered by the Building Regulations, but for further information see *Workplace health, safety and welfare, Workplace (Health, Safety and Welfare) Regulations 1992, Approved Code of Practice and guidance*, HSE publication L24, 1996.

3.30   Where the requirements of the Building Regulations that are covered by this Approved Document do not apply to **dwellings**, the provisions may still be required in the situations described above in order to satisfy the Workplace Regulations.

Section 4: Guidance relating to building work

THE EXTENSION OF A DWELLING

Reference method

Fabric standards

4.1 Reasonable provision would be for the proposed extension to incorporate the following:

a. newly constructed **thermal elements** that meet the standards set out in paragraphs 5.1 to 5.6;

b. doors, windows, roof windows and rooflights that meet the standards set out in paragraphs 4.19 to 4.23;

c. improvements to fabric elements that are to become **thermal elements**, following the guidance in paragraphs 5.6 to 5.11.

Area of windows, roof windows and doors

4.2 In most circumstances reasonable provision would be to limit the total area of windows, roof windows and doors in extensions so that it does not exceed the sum of:

a. 25 per cent of the floor area of the extension; plus

b. the total area of any windows or doors which, as a result of the extension works, no longer exist or are no longer exposed.

As a general guide, if the area of glazing is much less than 20 per cent of the total floor area, some parts of the extension and especially the part of the dwelling it covers may experience poor levels of daylight, resulting in increased use of electric lighting. Areas of glazing greater than 25 per cent may be acceptable, especially if this is required to make the extension consistent with the external appearance or character of the host building. In such cases and where practical, either the U-value of the window should be improved relative to the standard set out in paragraph 4.1b, or other compensating measures applied following the guidance set out in paragraphs 4.4 to 4.7.

Heating and lighting in the extension

4.3 Where a **fixed building service** is provided or extended as part of constructing the extension, reasonable provision would be to follow the guidance in paragraphs 4.24 to 4.37.

Optional approaches with more design flexibility

4.4 The approach set out in paragraphs 4.1 to 4.3 is somewhat prescriptive. The following paragraphs offer more flexible approaches to demonstrating that reasonable provision has been made. These alternative approaches allow some elements of the design to be relaxed through compensating measures elsewhere.

Area-weighted U-value method

4.5 One way of complying would be to show that the area-weighted U-value of all the elements in the extension is no greater than that of an extension of the same size and shape that complies with the fabric standards referred to in paragraph 4.1 and the opening area standards in paragraph 4.2. Any **fixed building service** provided or extended as part of constructing the extension should follow the guidance in paragraphs 4.24 to 4.37.

The area-weighted U-value is given by the following expression:

$$\{(U_1 \times A_1) + (U_2 \times A_2) + (U_3 \times A_3) + ...)\} \div \{(A_1 + A_2 + A_3 + ...)\}$$

Whole dwelling calculation method

4.6 Where even greater design flexibility is required, reasonable provision would be to use SAP 2012 to show that the calculated carbon dioxide (CO_2) emission rate from the **dwelling** with its proposed extension is no greater than for the **dwelling** plus a notional extension built to the standards of paragraphs 4.1 to 4.3. The openings in the notional extension should conform with paragraph 4.2 with door area set equal to the door area of the proposed extension, with the remainder of the openings being classified as windows. The data in SAP 2012 Appendix S can be used to estimate the performance of the elements of the existing building where these are unknown.

Approved Document C gives limiting values for individual elements to minimise condensation risk.

4.7 If, as part of achieving the standard set out in paragraph 4.6, upgrades are proposed to the existing **dwelling**, such upgrades should be implemented to a standard that is no worse than set out in the relevant guidance contained in this Approved Document. The relevant standards for improving retained **thermal elements** are as set out in column (b) of Table 3.

Where it is proposed to upgrade the original building, the standards set out in this Approved Document are cost-effective and should be implemented in full. It will be worthwhile implementing them even if the improvement is greater than necessary to achieve compliance. In some cases, therefore, the standard of the extended dwelling may be better than that required by paragraph 4.6 alone. Paragraph 4.7 sets limits on design flexibility and ensures that no cost-effective improvement opportunities are traded away.

Conservatories and porches

4.8 Where the extension is a conservatory or porch that is not exempt from the **energy efficiency requirements** (see paragraphs 3.15

and 3.16 above), then reasonable provision would be to provide:

a. Effective thermal separation between the heated area in the existing *dwelling*, i.e. the walls, doors, and windows between the *dwelling* and the extension, should be insulated and draught proofed to at least the same extent as in the existing *dwelling*.

b. Independent temperature and on/off controls to any heating system installed within the extension. Any *fixed building service* installed within the extension should also conform to the standards set out in paragraphs 4.24 to 4.37.

c. Glazed elements should meet the standards set out in Table 1 and opaque elements should meet the standards set out in Table 2. However, the limitations on total area of windows, roof windows and doors as set out at paragraph 4.2 above do not apply.

4.9 Removing, and not replacing, any or all of the thermal separation between the *dwelling* and an existing exempt extension, or extending the *dwelling's* heating system into the extension, means the extension ceases to be exempt (see paragraphs 3.15 and 3.16 above). In such situations, the extension should be treated as a conventional extension and reasonable provision would be to demonstrate that the extension meets the guidance set out in paragraphs 4.1 to 4.7 above.

Swimming pool basins

4.10 Where a swimming pool is being provided in a building, the U-value of the basin (walls and floor) should be not worse than 0.25 W/m².K as calculated according to BS EN ISO 13370[4].

Design consideration should be taken with regards to compressive creep, insulation boards not being fully supported and the effects of point loading. Care should be taken to avoid thermal bridging particularly around basin wall and floor junctions with foundations.

MATERIAL CHANGE OF USE AND CHANGE OF ENERGY STATUS

Material change of use

4.11 Material changes of use (see regulation 5 of the Building Regulations) covered by this document are where, after the change:

a. the building is used as a *dwelling*, where previously it was not;

b. the building contains a flat, where previously it did not; or

c. the building, which contains at least one *dwelling*, contains a greater or lesser number of *dwellings* than it did previously.

4 BS EN ISO 13370 Thermal performance of buildings – Heat transfer via the ground – Calculation methods [2007 incorporating corrigendum March 2009].

Change of energy status

4.12 A change to a building's energy status is defined in regulation 2(1) as:

> any change which results in a building becoming a building to which the energy efficiency requirements of these Regulations apply, where previously it was not.

4.13 The requirements relating to a change to energy status are in regulation 22:

> Where there is a change in a building's energy status, such work, if any, shall be carried out to ensure that the building complies with the applicable requirements of regulation 40 and Part L of Schedule 1.

4.14 In this regulation 'building' means the building as a whole or parts of the building that have been designed or altered to be used separately.

For example, this could occur where a previously unheated building, or parts of the building that have been designed or altered to be used separately, were to be heated in future, or where a previously exempt building were no longer within the exempted categories. A material alteration (regulation 3(2) and (3)) may result in a change in buildings energy status.

4.15 In normal circumstances, reasonable provision where there is a material change of use or a change to the building's energy status would be:

a. Where *controlled services or fittings* are being provided or extended, to meet the standards set out in paragraphs 4.17 to 4.37. If the area of openings in the newly created *dwelling* is more than 25 per cent of the total floor area, either the area of openings should be reduced to be not greater than 25 per cent, or the larger area should be compensated for in some other way using the procedure described in paragraph 4.16.

b. Where the work involves the provision of a *thermal element*, to meet the standards set out in paragraphs 5.1 to 5.6.

For the purposes of Building Regulations, provision means both new and replacement elements.

c. Where any *thermal element* is being retained, to upgrade it following the guidance given in paragraphs 5.11 to 5.13.

d. Where an existing window (including roof window or rooflight) or door which separates a conditioned space from an unconditioned space or the external environment has a U-value that is worse than 3.3 W/(m².K), to provide replacement units following the guidance in paragraphs 4.19 to 4.23.

Option providing more design flexibility

4.16 To provide more design flexibility, SAP 2012 can be used to demonstrate that the total CO_2 emissions from all the **dwellings** in the building as it will become are no greater than if each **dwelling** had been improved following the guidance set out in paragraph 4.15.

WORK ON CONTROLLED FITTINGS AND SERVICES

4.17 **Controlled services or fittings** are defined in regulation 2 as follows:

Controlled service or fitting means a service or fitting in relation to which Part G, H, J, L or P of Schedule 1 imposes a requirement;

Controlled fittings

4.18 In the context of this Approved Document, the application of the term **controlled fitting** to a window, roof window, rooflight or door refers to a whole unit, i.e. including the frame. Consequently, replacing the glazing whilst retaining an existing frame is not providing a **controlled fitting**, and so such work is not notifiable and does not have to meet the Part L standards, although where practical it would be sensible to do so. Similar arguments apply to doors, where the **controlled fitting** refers to the complete doorset (leaf plus frame). Replacing a door leaf whilst retaining the existing frame is not notifiable and does not have to meet the Part L standards, although where practical it would be sensible to do so.

4.19 Where windows, roof windows, rooflights or doors are to be provided, reasonable provision in normal cases would be the installation of draught-proofed units whose performance is no worse than given in Table 1. In addition, insulated cavity closers should be installed where appropriate. Where the windows or fully glazed external pedestrian doors are unable to meet the requirements of Table 1 because of the need to maintain the external appearance of the façade or the character of the building, such fittings should meet a centre pane U-value of 1.2 W/(m².K), where the centre-pane U-value is defined as the U-value determined in the central area of the glazing unit, making no allowance for edge spacers or window frame. As an alternative, single glazing should be supplemented with low-e secondary glazing. In this latter case, the weather stripping should be on the secondary glazing to minimise condensation risk between the primary and secondary glazing. Where enhanced performance requirements (e.g. wind load, safety, security or acoustic attenuation) require thicker glass to be used, reasonable provision would be demonstrated if the window unit with the equivalent standard glazing thickness can be shown to comply.

4.20 U-values shall be calculated using the methods and conventions set out in BR 443[5], and should be based on the whole unit (i.e. in the case of a window, the combined performance of the glazing and frame). The U-value of the window can be calculated for:

a. the smaller of the two standard windows defined in BS EN 14351-1[6]; or

b. the standard window configuration set out in BR 443; or

c. the specific size and configuration of the actual window.

The U-value of the door can be calculated for:

a. the standard size as laid out in BS EN 14351-1; or

b. the specific size and configuration of the actual door.

SAP 2012 Table 6e gives values for different window configurations that can be used in the absence of test data or calculated values.

4.21 The U-values for roof windows and rooflights given in this Approved Document are based on the U-value having been assessed with the roof window or rooflight in the vertical position. If a particular unit has been assessed in a plane other than the vertical, the standards given in this Approved Document should be modified by making an adjustment that is dependent on the slope of the unit following the guidance in BR 443.

Table 1 **Standards for controlled fittings[1]**

Fitting	Standard
Window, roof window or rooflight[2]	WER Band C or better (see paragraph 4.22), or U-value 1.6 W/(m².K)
Doors with >60% of internal face glazed	Doorset Energy Rating (DSER) Band E or better (see paragraph 4.22), or U-value 1.8 W/(m².K)
Other doors	DSER Band E or better (see paragraph 4.22), or U-value 1.8 W/(m².K)

Notes:

1. Since the U-values are determined for standard configurations (see paragraph 4.20), the effects of Georgian bars and/or leaded lights can be ignored.

2. For the purposes of checking compliance with this table, the true U-value based on aperture area can be converted to the U-value based on the developed area of the rooflight. Further guidance on evaluating the U-value of out-of-plane rooflights is given in Assessment of thermal performance of out-of-plane rooflights, NARM Technical Document NTD 2 (2010). See http://www.narm.org.uk/uploads/pdfs/NARM-TAOOPR-030311.pdf.

4.22 The calculation of Window Energy Rating (WER) and the Doorset Energy Rating (DSER) are set out in the GGF Guide to the Calculation of Energy Ratings for Windows,

---

5   BR 443 Conventions for U-value calculations, BRE, 2006.
6   BS EN 14351 1 Windows and doors – Product standard, performance characteristics. Windows and external pedestrian doorsets without resistance to fire and/or smoke leakage characteristics [2006 (+AMD 1:2010)].

Roof Windows and Doors[7]. The guide provides different procedures for windows, roof windows, external pedestrian doors and patio/French/sliding/folding doors. **BCBs** may accept a WER and/or DSER declaration from a certification scheme that provides a quality assured process and supporting audit trail from calculating the performance of the window through to installation as evidence of compliance. Notwithstanding the suggested performance values set out in Table 1, guidance on energy efficient windows is available from the Energy Saving Trust[8].

4.23 If a window is enlarged or a new one created, then the area of windows, roof windows, rooflights and doors should not exceed 25 per cent of the total floor area of the **dwelling** unless compensating measures are included elsewhere in the work.

Controlled services

4.24 Whenever a **fixed building service** is extended or provided, reasonable provision would be demonstrated by following the guidance set out in the *Domestic Building Services Compliance Guide*[9]. The Guide covers the following services:

a. heating and hot water systems (including insulation of pipes, ducts and vessels;

b. mechanical ventilation;

c. mechanical cooling/air-conditioning;

d. fixed internal lighting;

e. fixed external lighting;

f. renewable energy systems.

4.25 The efficiency claimed for the **fixed building service** should be based on the appropriate test standard as set out in the *Domestic Building Services Compliance Guide* and the test data should be certified by a notified body. It would be reasonable for **BCBs** to accept such data at face value. In the absence of such quality-assured data, **BCBs** should satisfy themselves that the claimed performance is justified.

4.26 When replacing an existing appliance, the efficiency of the new appliance should not be significantly less than the efficiency of the appliance being replaced. If the replacement involves a fuel switch, then the relative carbon emissions associated with the new and existing fuels should be considered when assessing the reasonableness of the proposed new appliance. The *Domestic Building Services Compliance Guide* contains the detailed guidance on this issue.

4.27 If a renewable energy generator such as a wind turbine or photovoltaic array is being replaced, the new system should have an electrical output that is not less than the original installation.

4.28 When replacing a heating appliance, consideration should be given to connecting to any existing local heat networks. If the work involves pipework changes, consideration should be given to providing capped off connections to facilitate subsequent connection to a planned local heat network.

4.29 If a particular technology is not covered in the *Domestic Building Services Compliance Guide*, reasonable provision would be demonstrated by showing that the proposed technology gives a performance that is no worse than a reference system of the same type whose details are given in the Guide.

COMMISSIONING OF FIXED BUILDING SERVICES

4.30 Paragraph L1(b)(iii) of Schedule 1 to the Building Regulations requires **fixed building services** to be commissioned by testing and adjustment as necessary to ensure that they use no more fuel and power than is reasonable in the circumstances. In order to demonstrate that the heating and hot water systems have been adequately commissioned, regulation 44 states:

44 Commissioning

(1) This regulation applies to building work in relation to which paragraph F1(2) of Schedule 1 imposes a requirement, but does not apply to the provision or extension of any fixed system for mechanical ventilation or any associated controls where testing and adjustment is not possible.

(2) This regulation applies to building work in relation to which paragraph L1(b) of Schedule 1 imposes a requirement, but does not apply to the provision or extension of any fixed building service where testing and adjustment is not possible or would not affect the energy efficiency of that fixed building service.

(3) Where this regulation applies the person carrying out the work shall, for the purpose of ensuring compliance with paragraph F1(2) or L1(b) of Schedule 1, give to the local authority a notice confirming that the fixed building services have been commissioned in accordance with a procedure approved by the Secretary of State.

(4) The notice shall be given to the local authority–

a. not later than the date on which the notice required by regulation 16(4) is required to be given; or

b. where that regulation does not apply, not more than 30 days after completion of the work.

---

[7] Guide to the Calculation of Energy Ratings for Windows, Roof Windows and Doors, GGF, 2013.

[8] www.energysavingtrust.org.uk/Insulation/Windows.

[9] Domestic Building Services Compliance Guide, DCLG, 2013.

4.31 Reasonable provision would be to prepare a *commissioning* plan, identifying the systems that need to be tested and the tests that will be carried out. The notice required by regulation 44 should confirm that the *commissioning* plan has been followed and that every system has been inspected in an appropriate sequence and to a reasonable standard and that the test results confirm that performance is reasonably in accordance with the design requirements.

4.32 Not all *fixed building services* will need to be commissioned. With some systems adjustment is not possible as the only controls are 'on' and 'off' switches. Examples of this would be some mechanical extraction systems or single fixed electrical heaters. In other cases *commissioning* would be possible but in the specific circumstances would have no effect on energy use.

Fixed building services which do not require commissioning should be identified in the commissioning plan, along with the reason for not requiring commissioning.

4.33 Where *commissioning* is carried out it must be done in accordance with a procedure approved by the Secretary of State. For heating and hot water systems the approved procedures are set out in the *Domestic Building Services Compliance Guide*. For ventilation systems, an approved procedure would be to follow the guidance in the *Domestic Ventilation Compliance Guide*[10].

4.34 *Commissioning* is often carried out by the person who installs the system. In other cases it may be carried out by a subcontractor or by a specialist firm. It is important that whoever carries it out follows the relevant approved procedure in doing so.

4.35 Where a building notice or full plans have been given to a local authority *BCB,* the notice of completion of *commissioning* should be given to that *BCB* within 5 days of the completion of the *commissioning* work. In other cases, for example where work is carried out by a person registered with a competent person scheme (see paragraphs 3.19 to 3.22), it must be given within 30 days.

4.36 Where an approved inspector is the *BCB*, the notice of completion of *commissioning* should generally be given to the approved inspector within 5 days of the completion of work. However, where the work is carried out by a person registered with a competent person scheme (see paragraph 3.19 to 3.22), the notice must be given within 30 days. Where the installation of *fixed building services* which require *commissioning* is carried out by a person registered with a competent person scheme the notice of *commissioning* will be given by that person.

4.37 Until the *BCB* receives the *commissioning* notice it cannot be reasonably satisfied that Part L has been complied with and consequently is unlikely to be able to give a completion/final certificate.

---

[10]   Domestic Ventilation Compliance Guide, DCLG, 2010.

Section 5: Guidance on thermal elements

5.1 New *thermal elements* must comply with Part L1(a)(i) of Schedule 1 to the Building Regulations. Work on existing *thermal elements* must comply with regulation 23 of the Building Regulations which states:

Requirements for the renovation or replacement of thermal elements – Regulation 23

(1) Where the renovation of an individual thermal element—

    (a) constitutes a major renovation; or

    (b) amounts to the renovation of more than 50% of the element's surface area;

    the renovation must be carried out so as to ensure that the whole of the element complies with paragraph L1(a)(i) of Schedule 1, in so far as that is technically, functionally and economically feasible.

(2) Where the whole or any part of an individual element is proposed to be replaced and the replacement—

    (a) constitutes a major renovation; or

    (b) (in the case of part replacement) amounts to the replacement of more than 50% of the thermal element's surface area;

    the whole of the thermal element must be replaced so as to ensure that it complies with paragraph L1(a)(i) of Schedule 1, in so far as that is technically, functionally and economically feasible.

THE PROVISION OF THERMAL ELEMENTS

U-values

5.2 U-values shall be calculated using the methods and conventions set out in BR 443.

5.3 Reasonable provision for newly constructed *thermal elements* such as those constructed as part of an extension would be to meet the standards set out in Table 2.

5.4 Reasonable provision for those *thermal elements* constructed as replacements for existing elements would be to meet the standards set out in Table 2.

Table 2 Standards for new thermal elements

Element[1]	Standard W/(m².K)[2]
Wall	0.28
Pitched roof – insulation at ceiling level	0.16
Pitched roof – insulation at rafter level	0.18
Flat roof or roof with integral insulation	0.18
Floors[3]	0.22[4]
Swimming pool basin	0.25

Notes:

1. 'Roof' includes the roof parts of dormer windows, and 'wall' includes the wall parts (cheeks) of dormer windows.

2. Area-weighted average values.

3. A lesser provision may be appropriate where meeting such a standard would result in a reduction of more than 5% in the internal floor area of the room bounded by the wall.

4. A lesser provision may be appropriate where meeting such a standard would create significant problems in relation to adjoining floor levels. The U-value of the floor of an extension can be calculated using the exposed perimeter and floor area of the whole enlarged dwelling.

Continuity of insulation and airtightness

5.5   The building fabric should be constructed so that there are no reasonably avoidable thermal bridges in the insulation layers caused by gaps within the various elements, at the joints between elements, and at the edges of elements such as those around window and door openings. Reasonable provision should also be made to reduce unwanted air leakage through the new envelope parts. The work should comply with all the requirements of Schedule 1, but particular attention should be paid to Parts F and J.

5.6   A suitable approach to showing the requirement has been achieved would be to adopt Accredited Construction Details at www.planningportal.gov.uk.

It is impractical to expect thermal bridge and temperature factor calculations for work in existing buildings.

Major renovation

5.6A   *Major renovation* means the renovation of a building where more than 25% of the surface area of the **building envelope** undergoes renovation. When assessing whether the area proportion constitutes a **major renovation** of a building, the surface area of the whole of the external **building envelope** should be taken into account i.e. external walls, floor, roof, windows, doors, roof windows and rooflights.

RENOVATION OF THERMAL ELEMENTS

5.7   For the purposes of this Approved Document, **renovation** of a **thermal element** through:

a.   the provision of a new layer means either of the following activities:

   i.   Cladding or rendering the external surface of the **thermal element**; or

   ii.   Dry-lining the internal surface of a **thermal element**.

b.   the replacement of an existing layer means either of the following activities:

   i.   Stripping down the element to expose the basic structural components (brick/ blockwork, timber/metal frame, joists, rafters, etc.) and then rebuilding to achieve all the necessary performance requirements. As discussed in paragraph 3.9, particular considerations apply to renovating elements of traditional construction; or

   ii.   Replacing the water proof membrane on a flat roof.

5.8   Where a **thermal element** is subject to a **renovation** through undertaking an activity listed in paragraph 5.7a or 5.7b, the performance of the whole of the **thermal element** should be improved to achieve or better the relevant U-value set out in column (b) of Table 3, provided the area to be renovated is greater than 50% of the surface of the individual **thermal element** or constitutes a **major renovation** where more than 25% of the surface area of the **building envelope** undergoes **renovation**.

5.8A   In relation to the renovation of individual thermal elements, when assessing the proportion of the surface area that is to be renovated, the area of the **thermal element** should be assessed as the area of each individual **thermal element**, not the area of all the elements of that type in the building. The area of each individual **thermal element** should also be interpreted in the context of whether the element is being renovated from inside or outside, e.g. if removing all the plaster finish from the inside of a solid brick wall, the area of the element is the area of external wall in the room. If removing external render, it is the area of the elevation in which that wall sits.

This means that if all the roofing on the flat roof of an extension is being stripped down, the area of the individual element is the 'roof area' of the extension, not the 'total roof area' of the dwelling. Similarly, if the rear wall of a single storey extension is being re-rendered externally, then the rear wall of the extension should be upgraded to the standards of Table 3 column (b), even if the renovation affected less than 50% of the total area of the building elevation when viewed from the rear. If plaster is being removed from a bedroom wall, the relevant area is the area of the external wall in the room, not the area of the external elevation which contains that wall section. This is because the marginal cost of dry-lining with insulated plasterboard rather than plain plasterboard is small.

When a building undergoes a major renovation this may represent an opportunity to consider and take into account the technical, environmental and economic feasibility of installing high-efficiency alternative systems.

5.9   If achievement of the relevant U-value set out in column (b) of Table 3 is not technically or functionally feasible or would not achieve a **simple payback** of 15 years or less, the element should be upgraded to the best standard that is technically and functionally feasible and which can be achieved within a **simple payback** of no greater than 15 years. Guidance on this approach is given in Appendix A.

5.10   When renovating **thermal elements**, the work should comply with all the requirements in Schedule 1, but particular attention should be paid to Parts F and J.

RETAINED THERMAL ELEMENTS

5.11   Part L of Schedule 1 to the Building Regulations applies to retained *thermal elements* in the following circumstances:

a.   where an existing *thermal element* is part of a building subject to a material change of use;

b.   where an existing element is to become part of the thermal envelope where previously it was not, e.g. as part of a loft or garage conversion where the space is now to be heated.

5.12   Reasonable provision would be to upgrade those *thermal elements* whose U-value is worse than the threshold value in column (a) of Table 3 to achieve the U-values given in column (b) of Table 3 provided this is technically, functionally and economically feasible. A reasonable test of economic feasibility is to achieve a *simple payback* of 15 years or less. Where the standard given in column (b) is not technically, functionally or economically feasible, then the *thermal element* should be upgraded to the best standard that is technically and functionally feasible and delivers a *simple payback* period of 15 years or less. Generally, this lesser standard should not be worse than 0.7 W/(m².K).

Examples of where lesser provision than column (b) might apply are where the thickness of the additional insulation might reduce usable floor area of any room by more than 5 per cent or create difficulties with adjoining floor levels, or where the weight of the additional insulation might not be supported by the existing structural frame.

5.13   When upgrading retained *thermal elements*, the work should comply with all the requirements in Schedule 1, but particular attention should be paid to Parts F and J.

Table 3 Upgrading retained thermal elements

Element[1]	(a) Threshold U-value W/(m²·K)[8]	(b) Improved U-value W/(m²·K)[8]
Wall – cavity insulation[2]	0.70	0.55
Wall – external or internal insulation[3]	0.70	0.30
Floor[4,5]	0.70	0.25
Pitched roof – insulation at ceiling level	0.35	0.16
Pitched roof – insulation between rafters[6]	0.35	0.18
Flat roof or roof with integral insulation[7]	0.35	0.18

1   'Roof' includes the roof parts of dormer windows and 'wall' includes the wall parts (cheeks) of dormer windows.

2   This applies only in the case of a wall suitable for the installation of cavity insulation. Where this is not the case, it should be treated as 'wall – external or internal insulation'.

3   A lesser provision may be appropriate where meeting such a standard would result in a reduction of more than 5% in the internal floor area of the room bounded by the wall.

4   The U-value of the floor of an extension can be calculated using the exposed perimeter and floor area of the whole enlarged building.

5   A lesser provision may be appropriate where meeting such a standard would create significant problems in relation to adjoining floor levels.

6   A lesser provision may be appropriate where meeting such a standard would create limitations on head room. In such cases, the depth of the insulation plus any required air gap should be at least to the depth of the rafters, and the thermal performance of the chosen insulant should be such as to achieve the best practicable U-value.

7   A lesser provision may be appropriate if there are particular problems associated with the load-bearing capacity of the frame or the upstand height.

8   Area-weighted average values.

Section 6: Consequential improvements to energy performance

6.1   Regulation 28 of the Building Regulations may require additional work to be undertaken to make an existing building more energy efficient when certain types of building work are proposed.

6.2   This requirement arises in existing buildings with a total useful floor area of over 1,000 m^2 where the proposed work consists of:

a. an extension;

b. the initial provision of any **fixed building service** (other than a renewable energy generator);

c. an increase to the installed capacity of any **fixed building service** (other than a renewable energy generator);

6.3   **Consequential improvements** should only be carried out to the extent that they are technically, functionally and economically feasible.

6.4   Only a relatively small number of existing **dwellings** will exceed 1,000 m^2 in size. Where there is doubt the **BCB** can be consulted for advice.

6.5   Technical guidance on achieving compliance with regulation 28 is not given in this Approved Document but where the regulation applies it is available in Approved Document L2B.

Section 7: Providing information

7.1   On completion of the work, in accordance with regulation 40, the owner of the *dwelling* should be provided with sufficient information about the building, the *fixed building services* and their operating and maintenance requirements so that the *dwelling* can be operated in such a manner as to use no more fuel and power than is reasonable in the circumstances. This requirement applies only to the work that has actually been carried out, e.g. if the work involves replacing windows, there is no obligation on the contractor to provide details on the operation of the heating system.

7.2   Where the work involves the provision of a new heating system, a way of complying would be to provide a suitable set of operating and maintenance instructions aimed at achieving economy in the use of fuel and power in terms that householders can understand in a durable format that can be kept and referred to over the service life of the system(s). The instructions should be directly related to the particular system(s) installed as part of the work that has been carried out.

7.3   Without prejudice to the need to comply with health and safety requirements, any instructions should explain to the occupier of the *dwelling* how to operate the system(s) efficiently. This should include:

a. the making of adjustments to timing, temperature and flow control settings;

b. what routine maintenance is needed to enable operating efficiency to be maintained at a reasonable level through the service live(s) of the system(s).

Appendix A: Work to thermal elements

1 Where the *renovation* of an individual *thermal element* constitutes a *major renovation*; or amounts to the *renovation* of more than 50% of the element's surface area, an opportunity exists for cost-effective insulation improvements to be undertaken at marginal additional cost. This appendix provides guidance on the cost-effectiveness of insulation measures when undertaking various types of work on a *thermal element*.

2 Table A1 sets out the circumstances and the level of performance that would be considered reasonable provision in ordinary circumstances. When dealing with existing *dwellings* some flexibility in the application of standards is necessary to ensure that the context of each scheme can be taken into account while securing, as far as possible, the reasonable improvement. The final column in Table A1 provides guidance on a number of specific issues that may need to be considered in determining an appropriate course of action. As part of this flexible approach, it will be necessary to take into account technical risk and practicality in relation to the *dwelling* under consideration and the possible impacts on any adjoining building. In general the proposed works should take account of:

a. the requirements of any other relevant parts of Schedule 1 to the Building Regulations;

b. the general guidance on technical risk relating to insulation improvements contained in BR 262[11];

c. for buildings falling within the categories set out in paragraphs 3.7 to 3.8, the guidance produced by English Heritage.

Where it is not reasonable in the context of the works project to achieve the performance set out in Table A1 the level of performance achieved should be as close to this as practically possible.

3 Table A1 incorporates, in outline form, examples of construction that would achieve the proposed performance, but designers are free to use any appropriate construction that satisfies the energy performance standard, so long as they do not compromise performance with respect to any other part of the Building Regulations.

4 General guidance is available from such sources as the Energy Saving Trust and relevant British Standards.

---

[11] BR 262 Thermal insulation: Avoiding risks, BRE, 2002.

Table A1 Cost-effective U-value targets when undertaking renovation works to thermal elements

Proposed works	Target U-value W/(m².K)	Typical construction	Comments (reasonableness, practicability and cost- effectiveness)
Pitched roof constructions[12]			
Renewal of roof covering – No living accommodation in the roof void – existing insulation (if any) at ceiling level. No existing insulation, existing insulation less than 50 mm, in poor condition, and/ or likely to be significantly disturbed or removed as part of the planned work	0.16	Provide loft insulation – 250 mm mineral fibre or cellulose fibre as quilt laid between and across ceiling joists or loose fill or equivalent	Assess condensation risk in roof space and make appropriate provision in accordance with the requirements of Part C relating to the control of condensation. Additional provision may be required to provide access to and insulation of services in the roof void
Renewal of roof covering – Existing insulation in good condition and will not be significantly disturbed by proposed works. Existing insulation thickness 50 mm or more but less than 100 mm	0.16	Top up loft insulation to at least 250 mm mineral fibre or cellulose fibre as quilt laid between and across ceiling joists or loose fill or equivalent. This may be boarded out	Assess condensation risk in roof space and make appropriate provision in line with the requirements of Part C relating to the control of condensation. Additional provision may be required to provide insulation and access to services in the roof void Where the loft is already boarded out and the boarding is not to be removed as part of the work, the practicality of insulation works would need to be considered
Renewal of the ceiling to cold loft space. Existing insulation at ceiling level removed as part of the works	0.16	Provide loft insulation – 250 mm mineral fibre or cellulose fibre as quilt laid between and across ceiling joists or loose fill or equivalent. This may be boarded out	Assess condensation risk in roof space and make appropriate provision in accordance with the requirements of Part C relating to the control of condensation. Additional provision may be required to provide insulation and access to services in the roof void Where the loft is already boarded out and the boarding is not to be removed as part of the work, insulation can be installed from the underside but the target U-value may not be achievable
Renewal of roof covering – Living accommodation in roof space (room-in- the-roof type arrangement), with or without dormer windows	0.18	Cold structure – Insulation (thickness dependent on material) placed between and below rafters Warm structure – Insulation placed between and above rafters	Assess condensation risk (particularly interstitial condensation), and make appropriate provision in accordance with the requirements of Part C relating to the control of condensation (Clause 8.4 of BS 5250:2002 and BS EN ISO 13788:2002 Practical considerations with respect to an increase in structural thickness (particularly in terraced dwellings) may necessitate a lower performance target
Dormer window constructions			
Renewal of cladding to side walls	0.30	Insulation (thickness dependent on material) placed between and/or fixed to outside of wall studs. Or fully external to existing structure depending on construction	Assess condensation risk and make appropriate provision in accordance with the requirements of Part C
Renewal of roof covering	–	Follow guidance on improvement to pitched or flat roofs as appropriate	Assess condensation risk and make appropriate provision in accordance with the requirements of Part C

Table A1 Cost-effective U-value targets when undertaking renovation works to thermal elements

Proposed works	Target U-value W/(m².K)	Typical construction	Comments (reasonableness, practicability and cost- effectiveness)
Flat roof constructions			
Renewal of roof covering – Existing insulation, if any, less than 100 mm, mineral fibre (or equivalent resistance) or in poor condition and likely to be significantly disturbed or removed as part of the planned work	0.18	Insulation placed between and over joists as required to achieve the target U-value – Warm structure	Assess condensation risk and make appropriate provision in accordance with the requirements of Part C. Also see BS 6229:2003 for design guidance
Renewal of the ceiling to flat roof area. Existing insulation removed as part of the works	0.18	Insulation placed between and to underside of joists to achieve target U-value	Assess condensation risk and make appropriate provision in accordance with the requirements of Part C. Also see BS 6229:2003 for design guidance. Where ceiling height would be adversely affected, a lower performance target may be appropriate
Solid wall constructions			
Renewal of internal finish to external wall or applying a finish for the first time	0.30	Dry-lining to inner face of wall – insulation between studs fixed to wall to achieve target U-value – thickness dependent on insulation and stud material used	Assess the impact on internal floor area. In general it would be reasonable to accept a reduction of no more than 5% in the area of a room. However, the use of the room and the space requirements for movement and arrangements of fixtures, fittings and furniture should be assessed
		Insulated wall board fixed to internal wall surface to achieve the required U-value – thickness dependent on material used	In situations where acoustic attenuation issues are particularly important (e.g. where insulation is returned at party walls) a less demanding U-value may be more appropriate. In such cases, the U-value target may have to be increased to 0.35 or above depending on the circumstances
			Assess condensation and other moisture risks and make appropriate provision in accordance with the requirements of Part C. This will usually require the provision of a vapour control and damp protection to components. Guidance on the risks involved is provided in BR 262 and, on the technical options, in Energy Saving Trust publications
Renewal of finish or cladding to external wall area or elevation (render or other cladding) or applying a finish or cladding for the first time	0.30	External insulation system with rendered finish or cladding to give required U-value	Assess technical risk and impact of increased wall thickness on adjoining buildings
Ground floor constructions			
Renovation of a solid or suspended floor involving the replacement of screed or a timber floor deck	See comment	Solid floor – replace screed with an insulated floor deck to maintain existing floor level. Suspended timber floor – fit insulation between floor joists prior to replacement of floor deck	The cost-effectiveness of floor insulation is complicated by the impact of the size and shape of the floor (perimeter/area ratio). In many cases existing un-insulated floor U-values are already relatively low when compared with wall and roof U-values. Where the existing floor U-value is greater than 0.70 W/(m².K), then the addition of insulation is likely to be cost-effective. Analysis shows that the cost–benefit curve for the thickness of added insulation is very flat, and so a target U-value of 0.25 W/(m².K) is appropriate subject to other technical constraints (adjoining floor levels, etc.)

[12] Specification of thickness of insulation is based on lambda values (conductivity) of 0.04 W/(m.K).

Appendix B: Documents referred to

BRE

www.bre.co.uk

BR 262 *Thermal insulation: avoiding risks* (2002 Edition) printed in 2006. ISBN 978 186081 515 4

BRE Report BR 443 *Conventions for U-value calculations*, 2006. (Available at www.bre.co.uk/uvalues)

Department for Business, Innovation and Skills

www.bis.gov.uk

Technical Standards and Regulations Directive 98/34/EC. (Available at www.bis.gov.uk/policies/innovation/infrastructure/Standardisation/tech-standards-directive)

Department of Energy and Climate Change (DECC)

www.decc.gov.uk

The Government's Standard Assessment Procedure for energy rating of dwellings, SAP 2012. (Available at www.bre.co.uk/sap2012)

Current Energy Prices (www.gov.uk/government/organisations/department-of-energy-climate-change/about/statistics#energy-price-statistics)

Department for Communities and Local Government (DCLG)

www.communities.gov.uk

Accredited Construction Details for Part L (Available to download from www.planningportal.gov.uk/england/professionals/en/1115314255826.html)

Energy Saving Trust (EST)

www.est.org.uk

Energy Efficient Glazing – guidance (Available at www.energysavingtrust.org.uk/Home-improvements-and-products/Home-insulation-glazing/Glazing)

English Heritage

www.english-heritage.org.uk

Energy Efficiency and Historic Buildings, English Heritage, 2011.

Glass and Glazing Federation (GGF)

www.ggf.org.uk

Guide to the Calculation of Energy Ratings for Windows, Roof Windows and Doors, GGF, 2013.

Health and Safety Executive (HSE)

www.hse.gov.uk

L24 Workplace Health, Safety and Welfare: Workplace (Health, Safety and Welfare) Regulations1992, Approved Code of Practice and Guidance, The Health and Safety Commission 1992. ISBN 978 0 71760 413 5

National Association of Rooflight Manufacturers (NARM)

www.narm.org.uk

NARM Technical Document NTD 2, 2010.

NBS (on behalf of the Department for Communities and Local Government)

www.thebuildingregs.com

Domestic Building Services Compliance Guide, DCLG, 2013.

Domestic Ventilation Compliance Guide, DCLG, 2010.

(Both available to download from www.planningportal.gov.uk)

Legislation

Ancient Monuments and Archaeological Areas Act 1979

Listed Buildings and Conservation Areas) Act 1990

SI 2010/2214 The Building Regulations 2010

SI 2010/2215 The Building (Approved Inspectors etc.) Regulations 2010

Appendix C: Standards referred to

BS EN ISO 13370 Thermal performance of buildings – Heat transfer via the ground – Calculation methods [2007 incorporating corrigendum March 2009].

BS EN 14351-1 Windows and doors – Product standard, performance characteristics. Windows and external pedestrian doorsets without resistance to fire and/or smoke leakage characteristics [2006 (+AMD 1:2010)].

BS 5250:2002 Code of practice for control of condensation in buildings.

BS EN ISO 13788:2002 Hygrothermal performance of building components and building elements.

BS 6229:2003 Flat roofs with continuously supported coverings. Code of practice.